Guess Who's in the
Snow

Picture credits
(t=top, b=bottom, l=left, r=right, c=centre, fc=front cover)
FLPA: 6–7 Michael Quinton/Minden Pictures; 8–9, 16–17 Matthias Breiter/
Minden Pictures; 12–13 Jurgen & Christine Sohns; 14–15 Theo Allofs/Minden Pictures;
18–19 Hiroya Minakuci/Minden Pictures
Nature PL: 10–11 Jenny E. Ross
Shutterstock: fc FloridaStock; 3 Erni; 4–5 Eric Isselee

Editor: Ruth Symons
Cover Designer: Krina Patel
Editorial Director: Victoria Garrard
Art Director: Laura Roberts-Jensen

Copyright © QED Publishing 2014

First published in the UK in 2014 by
QED Publishing, a Quarto Group company
The Old Brewery, 6 Blundell Street
London N7 9BH

www.qed-publishing.co.uk

A catalogue record for this book is available from the British Library.

ISBN 978 1 78171 539 0

Printed in China

Guess Who's in the Snow

Snow

Camilla De La Bédoyère and Fiona Hajée

QED

QED Publishing

Who has
black skin and
white fur?

Who loves to
tumble and roll
in the snow?

Who lives with
Mum and a twin?

Who has
huge
antlers?

Who has fur that can change colour?

Who has a bushy tail?

Who sleeps in
a snow den?

Who has fluffy
white fur and big
black eyes?

Who is good
at hiding?

Who flies silently?

Who has long
white ears with
black tips?

Who lives in the coldest
place in the world?

Who has grey
fluffy feathers?